By the *Alchimiste*

Matthias Giroud

With a preface by Pierre Gagnaire
Translated from the French by Katherine Gregor

LOW & NO ALCOHOL COCKTAILS

Hardie Grant

BOOKS

Written by
Matthias Giroud

Photographed and designed by
**Valéry Guedes
and Élisabeth Guedes**

The author wishes to thank
Mélinda Guerin-White
for her invaluable input

MATTHIAS GIROUD

Recognised worldwide by mixology enthusiasts, Matthias Giroud began his career in 1998 at Bar Fly in Paris, before moving on to work as bar manager at Bound, Buddha-Bar, Barrio Latino and Barlotti in Paris. In 2008, he took over responsibility for the world development of the bar for the entire George V Eatertainment Group (including the Buddha-Bar). He finally opened his own place in 2020, which is a combination of an artist's studio, chef's kitchen, herbalist and experience bar: L'Alchimiste.

Preface

Matthias Giroud is one of the leaders of a movement you could call 'the new bar art' just as 'nouvelle cuisine' was in its day.

He is the very incarnation of what we now call mixology – too technical a word for my taste – but which conveys the work carried out in search of aromas and flavours imagined the way a cook would imagine them while preparing a lobster or a vegetable dish.

Away with the rows of alcohol bottles, which, of course, still play their role, although no longer the lead.

Make room for infusing, macerating, decocting and concentrating.

The resulting drinks reflect the man's talent and sensitivity.

As a cook, I am hugely interested in this process: my entire culinary purpose is to offer a range of identifiable products, which, because of the way they are transformed, provide new flavours and textures that lead people to unpredictable horizons for the taste buds, with emotion as the operative word.

In this book, Matthias offers a highly interesting version of cocktails, since he sets aside all strong spirits.

His gentle approach provides a treat that does not eventually prevent a more classical enjoyment.

What makes this process fascinating is the true creativity that makes it possible to explore totally virgin lands and, as far as this book is concerned, to spoil yourself without needing to forego a second drink!

Matthias is a professional who teaches and has a passion for communication, as well as a genuine interest in other people.

His professionalism will not be contradicted by this book, and I can assure you that all his recipes will surprise you and produce cocktails bursting with flavours and cheer.

Pierre Gagnaire

CONTENTS

Introduction

**The cocktails. The bars.
The night. The party.
Yes, but (above all)...
not just that!** For some years now, the world of mixology has been in full swing. We have gone from traditional early- or late-evening cocktails (cosmopolitans, mojitos, and gin and tonics) to the era of liquid cuisine. The bar world is increasingly inspired by gastronomical tendencies and techniques loved by chefs: infusing, decocting, macerating, smoking, straining... and, more recently, extracting and fermenting. This book will introduce you to several incredibly delicious recipes, some nice and easy, others unexpected and possibly even wacky. Some require a bit of practice and equipment, while others are perfectly suitable for everyday life.

Matthias Giroud Trained in mixology with a CAP professional qualification, with distinction, in bar preparations, and with several trips under his belt, the *Alchimiste* developed a passion for the world of cocktails and honed his style. After a lengthy experience in the Buddha Bar group (for about 20 years, with as many countries visited and bars launched worldwide), Matthias finally settled in the Île-de-France with his business partner and friend Mélinda in order to start a true research and development laboratory for an entirely revamped cocktail offering. Matthias goes beyond the sector's codes and customs – strong spirits, tonics and sugar-heavy flavours – and imagines a range of cocktails devised as taste journeys where nature hobnobs with products close to its heart: spices, bark, flowers, roots, seasonings... all the gustatory, multisensorial palettes he now offers us in order to create extraordinarily exciting cocktails.

No low : quèsaco? Perhaps you're still unfamiliar with this jargon. *No low* is short for the world of cocktails without (no) alcohol or little (low) alcohol. Exit the concoctions that make your head spin after two sips and those that confuse your palate with too many flavours at once. What we have here is the world of mildness, of skill and of parallel options. Matthias proposes a moderate view of mixology. Therefore – promised – even if you're not going to take out all your bottles of rum, gin and whisky to make these 60 drinks, you will be able to treat yourself by (re)discovering various bottles in your cupboards and by letting other, less well-known, ingredients speak. Make room for verjuice, homemade juices, wines, Champagne, of course, but also teas, barks, flowers, herbal distillates and other essential oils. Don't panic: you don't have to purchase the entire barman's range to enjoy your drinks. There are recipes that will allow you to start gently, like the Basque Snack (page 68) or the Tramonto (page 154), which are more reassuring.

Travelling as a signature In the days of his multiple world travels, Matthias enjoyed spending hours discovering local produce, preparation techniques and the smells in the heart of the city... everything that makes a destination unique and bewitching and helps create memories that cannot be caught on film. After creating this sensory library, Matthias returns to his workshop and devises signature drinks no one had thought of. These nectars mark a place, an era and autograph life moments. As he devotes hours to trying out new blends and preparing potions to which only he knows the secret, he is soon nicknamed '*l'Alchimiste*' – a reference to the laboratory professionals who work excitedly in the highest secrecy.

24-hour enjoyment The mixologist quickly comes to face the facts: cocktails must not be restricted to the world of the night and alcohol. He attempts recipes that favour herbal infusions, fruit decoctions, spice macerations and daring juice blends. Cocktails around the clock. Morning citrus juices rub shoulders with the scents of verjuices, and homemade tonics marry essential oils. No hour of the day goes by without the opportunity to discover a divine concoction. Sampling Morning Himalaya (page 28) is to yield to the Far-Eastern encounter between ginger and Darjeeling tea. Continuing the day with Fleurs de France (page 47) is to dive into the landscapes of Provence, into fields of lavender... Take a nap and wake up to La Belle Hélène (page 74), in homage to the classic dessert.

The aperitif, often the unmissable time for cocktails, forms the exquisite Red Sylph (page 120) and its elderflower-strawberry-Champagne notes. You can have A Midsummer Night's Dream (page 158) by continuing the summer chords with the Champagne-rosemary duo. At nightfall, take your time simply with Almond Sour (page 187).

Creativity and method With these 60 recipes you will reach the Holy Grail. Here, Matthias gives you his lucky-charm, unmissable techniques that will allow you to produce a cordial, a homemade soda and even a herbal infusion. He also gives you 60 original, tasty and alluring mixtures suitable for all audiences and all uses. Equally, there are useful tips and knacks for decorating your glasses, successful straining, key syrups and macerations for developing your bartender list at home. Going a little further, Matthias provides clear steps so that you can understand all his techniques. You will also find templates for the *Alchimiste's* lucky-charm products: his favourite flowers, his unmissable roots, his essential oils... and even his bark. The two key words of his repertory are *curiosity* and *audacity*. For Matthias, every opportunity to discover a new product, every chance to sample a new spice and every trip (even to the end of the street) is a source of inspiration. Do the same. These recipes are skilfully studied so as to reveal the flavours of all their components with balance and precision, but feel free to dare and try out your own blends.

Matthias guides you through this collection, but he does not hinder your creativity – on the contrary: experiment, sample and, above all, enjoy!

MORNING ROUTINE

FROM 6 A.M. TO 12 P.M.

Between sweetness and energy

RISING SUN

The sun rises, the gentle morning warmth pervades our senses, which fly east around a smooth, delicate marriage of green tea and invigorating mango.

Makes 1 glass

200 ml (7 fl oz) soya milk
1 teaspoon Matcha tea
20 ml (1½ tablespoons) homemade mango honey

RECIPE

Pour the soya milk, Matcha tea and mango honey into a shaker. Shake, then double strain into a glass. Garnish.

FOR THE GARNISH

1 teaspoon Matcha tea powder

MANGO HONEY

100 ml (3½ fl oz) honey • 100 ml (3½ fl oz) mineral water
200 g (7 oz) fresh mango

Mix the honey and water, heated to 60°C (160°F), in a large bowl. Add the mango and mash with a fork. Infuse for 24 hours, then strain.
Will keep in the fridge for 1 week maximum.

A STROLL THROUGH THE PALM GROVE

Who has never dreamt of waking up in the middle of a luxuriant garden of palm trees and aromatic plants? I suggest you start the day with this refreshing trip.

Makes 1 glass

150 ml (5 fl oz) orange juice
10 ml (⅔ tablespoon) peppermint hydrolate
3 large ice cubes
150 ml (5 fl oz) pomegranate kombucha

RECIPE

Pour the orange juice and peppermint hydrolate into a glass, fill with the ice cubes and add the kombucha. Garnish.

FOR THE GARNISH

3 sprigs of fresh mint
1 handful of pomegranate seeds

ICED SALT CARAMEL MACCHIATO

The name alone suggests a leisurely breakfast: the sweetness of caramel, the roundness of oat milk, as well as the tanginess of coffee and its share of good vibes for the day: let's go!

Makes 1 glass

2 shots of espresso (freshly made)
300 ml (10 fl oz) oat milk
10 ml (⅔ tablespoon) salt caramel syrup (Monin brand)
2 large ice cubes

RECIPE

Pour the coffee, 300 ml (10 fl oz) of the oat milk and caramel syrup into a shaker. Shake vigorously, without the ice cubes, to dilute the caramel sauce well. Add the ice cubes and shake again, then double strain into the glass without the ice cubes.

Make the milk foam with the help of a milk frother. Complete with the milk foam and garnish.

FOR THE GARNISH

caramel sweets

PAINTING THE GLASS

I like to include artistic techniques in the world of mixology. We are going to 'paint' a glass in order to create a visual signature and a new tasting experience.

Dip a paintbrush into a jar of clear honey (to make it stickier you can blend honey with glucose syrup). Draw a line of honey on the glass, brushing several times to spread it evenly (dip the paintbrush in the honey only once for a thin coat).

Gently dust the honey with the powder of your choice (to make hibiscus powder, blend dried hibiscus flowers in a coffee grinder; you can use the same technique with all dried products). Once the powder is spread evenly, gently tap on the glass to remove any excess, and it's ready. You will have a visual signature and also be able to sample the cocktail with your lips touching the honey and powder as you drink.

Naturally, choose ingredients that have a connection with your cocktail. I provide a few suggestions in the recipes, in the Cloud of Flavour, for instance (page 30).

PUFF IN A MUG

A pure treat. You need 100% chocolate for this cocktail to be enjoyed, instead of traditional hot chocolate... but keeping the cookie, right?

Makes 1 mug

200 ml (7 fl oz) coconut milk
20 g (¾ oz) dark chocolate, broken into pieces
10 ml (⅔ tablespoon) dark chocolate sauce
1 small jar of homemade chocolate cookie foam

RECIPE

In a saucepan, heat the coconut milk and chocolate until the chocolate melts, add the chocolate sauce and stir. Fill a mug (I suggest you serve this cocktail in a cup and not in a glass) and lay the foam on the top. Garnish.

FOR THE GARNISH

pieces of good quality cookie (I love the ones made by Michel et Augustin)

CHOCOLATE COOKIE FOAM

200 ml (7 fl oz) almond or full-fat milk • 30 ml (1 fl oz) chocolate cookie syrup (Monin make a very good one)

Mix the ingredients and pour them into a syphon. Use one gas cartridge to make the mousse.
Will keep in the fridge for 3 days maximum.

CITRUS COFFEE

An unmissable breakfast partnership: a squeezed orange and a coffee – a good combination to start your day. What I propose here is something of a surprise... if not an uprise!

Makes 1 glass

20 ml (1½ tablespoons) pink grapefruit liqueur
10 ml (⅔ tablespoon) orange peel liqueur
20 ml (1½ tablespoons) lemon juice
6 large ice cubes
90 ml (3 fl oz) homemade cascara tonic

RECIPE

Pour the liqueurs and lemon juice into a glass, add the ice cubes and finish off with the cascara tonic. Garnish.

FOR THE GARNISH

slices of caramelised lemon (see method on page 39)

CASCARA TONIC

500 ml (17 fl oz) tonic water • 10 g (½ oz) cascara

Mix the ingredients and infuse in the fridge for 24 hours, then double strain.
Gasify the concoction with a soda syphon to obtain more bubbles.
Will keep in the fridge for 1 week maximum.

MORNING HIMALAYA

Let us continue our sensory journey towards the East and pause to admire this magnificent mountain.

Makes 1 glass

5 ml (1 teaspoon) almond syrup
10 ml (⅔ tablespoon) Timur berry cordial (Monin-Paragon brand)
30 ml (1 fl oz) ginger liqueur
6 large ice cubes
200 ml (7 fl oz) homemade Darjeeling and passion fruit soda
2 handfuls of crushed ice

RECIPE

Pour the almond syrup, Timur berry cordial and ginger liqueur into a shaker. Shake, without ice cubes, then pour into a glass filled with ice cubes. Complete with the soda and crushed ice. Garnish.

FOR THE GARNISH

fresh and crystallised ginger

DARJEELING AND PASSION FRUIT SODA

5 g (1¼ teaspoons) Darjeeling tea • 40 g (1½ oz) passion fruit flesh • 500 ml (17 fl oz) mineral water

Place the ingredients in a carafe and infuse in the fridge for 24 hours, then double strain.
Pour the concoction into a soda syphon and gasify it. Will keep in the fridge for 1 week maximum.

CLOUD OF FLAVOUR

Fruit, the sweetness of homemade almond milk, the mildness of rooibos... truly sublime.

Makes 1 glass

200 ml (7 fl oz) homemade pineapple juice infused with vanilla rooibos tea
30 ml (1 fl oz) apricot liqueur
5 large ice cubes
1 small jar of homemade almond milk foam

RECIPE

Pour the pineapple juice and apricot liqueur into a shaker. Add the ice cubes and shake. Strain into a glass and add the almond milk foam. Garnish.

FOR THE GARNISH

15 ml (1 tablespoon) dried apricot 'paint' (see method on page 21)
a few grams of vanilla rooibos tea

PINEAPPLE JUICE INFUSED WITH VANILLA ROOIBOS TEA

500 ml (17 fl oz) fresh pineapple juice
5 g (1¼ teaspoons) rooibos tea

Infuse the pineapple juice with the tea in the fridge for 24 hours, then strain and put aside.
  Will keep in the fridge for 1 week maximum.

ALMOND MILK FOAM

200 ml (7 fl oz) almond milk · 15 ml (1 tablespoon) agave syrup

Mix the ingredients and pour into a syphon. Use two gas cartridges to make the foam.
  Will keep in the fridge for 3 days maximum.

THE WORLD
OF LEAVES

Focus on
Verbena

What is it?   It is an aromatic and decorative plant that contains over a hundred species. People used to attribute therapeutic properties to it. I like classic verbena – everyone is familiar with its famous after-dinner infusions – as well as lemon verbena, refreshing and summery.

Did you know?   There is a variety called Argentinian vervain that has notes of mint and mandarin.

Its flavour in three words   Fresh + heady + citrusy.

How I use it   Just like berries, I love using infused verbena. This way, it releases its fresh minty and citrusy aromas. I find that it blends perfectly with many other flavours, like in the Parfum de France recipe (page 103), where it makes a perfect match with blackcurrant. When I think of verbena, I think of summer, of the scents of southern France, but equally of Asia's signatures, such as lemongrass and citrus fruits.

My other favourite leaves   I very much like using fruit tree leaves, like fig leaves. They are aesthetically splendid and are also a great asset to cooking with their deeply floral jasmine notes. Another leaf dear to my taste buds is the shiso leaf, also very attractive with its serrated edges; its taste is something between mint, cinnamon, cumin and parsley: complex and rather unusual. You can find it increasingly easily in exotic grocery shops.

JAPAN DETOX

The stroll towards the East continues...
The intoxicating aromas of Japan fly over this
cocktail that is all energy and vibration. It gives
the day a peppy, well-organised start.

Makes 1 glass

15 ml (1 tablespoon) lemon juice
5 ml (1 teaspoon) yuzu juice
10 ml (⅔ tablespoon) fresh ginger juice
10 ml (⅔ tablespoon) agave syrup
3 large ice cubes
120 ml (4 fl oz) homemade green tea and cherry blossom soda

RECIPE

Pour the lemon, yuzu and ginger juices and the agave syrup into a glass, add the ice cubes and complete with the soda. Garnish.

FOR THE GARNISH

edible white flowers
lemon zest

GREEN TEA AND CHERRY BLOSSOM SODA

5 g (1¼ teaspoons) green tea with cherry blossom (the Palais des Thés brand is perfect) • 500 ml (17 fl oz) mineral water • 20 ml (1½ tablespoons) agave syrup

Make a cold infusion: leave the tea to infuse in the water in the fridge for 24 hours, then double strain. Add the agave syrup, stir, then gasify the concoction with a soda syphon.
  Will keep in the fridge for 1 week maximum.

FRENCH BELLINI

My version of the famous Bellini: an unmissable cocktail with a twist of buckwheat that will astonish your guests.

Makes 1 glass

20 ml (1½ tablespoons) homemade buckwheat and peach liqueur
30 ml (1 fl oz) peach purée
5 large ice cubes
90 ml (3 fl oz) dry cider

RECIPE

Pour the liqueur and peach purée into a mixing glass, add the ice cubes and stir. Strain into a serving glass, without the ice cubes, and add the cider. Garnish.

FOR THE GARNISH

peach leather (see method on page 199)

BUCKWHEAT AND PEACH LIQUEUR

200 ml (7 fl oz) peach liqueur • 40 g (1½ oz) toasted buckwheat

Make a cold infusion: mix the ingredients at room temperature and let them rest for 24 hours, then double strain.
   Will keep at room temperature indefinitely.

QUICK FRUIT
CARAMELISING

A new experience inspired by pastry making, one-minute fruit caramelising acts on three senses: sight, taste and smell.

This technique is used with lemons on page 25. Place fresh lemon slices as a garnish on the glass. Sprinkle with brown sugar then caramelise gently with a mini-blowtorch – and voilà!

Do not hesitate to play with other ingredients. such as grapefruit, oranges or apples, and quickly caramelise them. You can also use brown sugar infused with vanilla, cinnamon or other ingredients.

BRUNCH BUBBLES

Brunch often goes in tandem with Champagne and we're not about to break this golden rule. Discover my version of the ideal cocktail to accompany a successful brunch.

Makes 1 glass

20 ml (1½ tablespoons) homemade chamomile cordial
20 ml (1½ tablespoons) raspberry purée
ice cubes
200 ml (7 fl oz) Champagne
1 squirt of chamomile spray

RECIPE

Pour the chamomile cordial and raspberry purée into a shaker. Shake with the ice cubes, then double strain into a glass. Add the Champagne and stir. Add a squirt of chamomile spray. Garnish.

FOR THE GARNISH

fresh white flowers
fresh raspberries

CHAMOMILE CORDIAL

500 ml (17 fl oz) mineral water • 300 g (10½ oz) caster (superfine) sugar • 6 g fresh (or dried) chamomile

Bring the water to the boil in a saucepan, add the sugar and keep on the heat until you have obtained a syrup. Turn off the heat, add the chamomile and cover with a lid. Leave to infuse for 30 minutes, then strain.

Will keep at room temperature for 2 weeks maximum.

COCKTAIL
LUNCH

FROM 12 P.M. TO 4 P.M.
Pleasure and measure

RASPBERRY CHARM

Blushing with pleasure – the pleasure of discovering a raspberry under its alluring dress with this refreshing cocktail. Do not hesitate to alter this recipe with your favourite seasonal fruit.

Makes 1 glass

30 ml (1 fl oz) homemade raspberry shrub
90 ml (3 fl oz) homemade wild mint and raspberry infusion
5 large ice cubes
60 ml (2 fl oz) good-quality tonic water

RECIPE

Pour the raspberry shrub and the mint and raspberry infusion into a glass filled with the ice cubes. Add the tonic water and stir. Garnish.

FOR THE GARNISH

small shoots of fresh mint
raspberries

RASPBERRY SHRUB

200 g (7 oz) raspberries · 200 g (7 oz) caster (superfine) sugar · 100 ml (3½ fl oz) cider vinegar

Put the raspberries and sugar into a mixing bowl. Mash, cover and leave to infuse for 24 hours. Transfer to a mixer, add the vinegar and blend.
Will keep in the fridge for 2 weeks maximum.

WILD MINT AND RASPBERRY INFUSION

5 g (1¼ teaspoons) dried mint · 150 g (5½ oz) raspberries · 500 ml (17 fl oz) mineral water

Prepare a cold infusion: put the mint and raspberries into a mixing bowl, crush them and add the water. Leave to infuse for 24 hours, then strain.
Will keep in the fridge for 1 week maximum.

FLEURS DE FRANCE

Provence, cicadas and vineyards... Can you picture the landscape of writer Marcel Pagnol? With this cocktail I am taking you south – are you ready?

Makes 1 glass

100 ml (3½ fl oz) Château Fontarèche white wine
20 ml (1½ tablespoons) Pêche de vigne (literally 'peach of the grapevine')
gin liqueur (Maison Villevert brand)
5 ml (1 teaspoon) lavender hydrolate
10 ml (⅔ tablespoon) verjuice

RECIPE

Pour all the ingredients into a mixing glass.
Stir and strain. Garnish.

FOR THE GARNISH

lavender flowers
5 ml (1 teaspoon) lavender 'paint'
(see method on page 21)

SANOVA

*We are bound for Italy with this alluring mixture...
It contains red vermouth, very sweet aromatic wine
which really takes off with the help of chinotto, a
citrus fruit similar to a bitter orange.*

Makes 1 glass

20 ml (1½ tablespoons) homemade balsamic strawberry shrub
40 ml (1¼ fl oz) red vermouth
20 ml (1½ tablespoons) bergamot juice
100 ml (3½ fl oz) chinotto
4–5 large ice cubes

RECIPE

Pour the shrub (you can strain it once more
before use) into a glass, then add the other
ingredients. Garnish.

FOR THE GARNISH

strawberries

BALSAMIC STRAWBERRY SHRUB

*200 g (7 oz) strawberries · 200 g (7 oz) caster
(superfine) sugar · 100 ml (3½ fl oz) dark balsamic
vinegar*

*Mix the strawberries and sugar by mashing them
roughly, then let everything macerate at room
temperature for 3 days. Add the balsamic vinegar
and strain.*

    Will keep in the fridge for 2 weeks maximum.

SUMBAWA

Are you familiar with makrut lime? It's a small citrus fruit that looks like a lime and tastes a little like lemongrass. It is very popular in Oriental cuisine.

Makes 1 glass

40 ml (1¼ fl oz) homemade raspberry liqueur with makrut lime oil
30 ml (1 fl oz) pink grapefruit juice
5 large ice cubes
120 ml (4 fl oz) good-quality wheat beer

RECIPE

Mix the raspberry liqueur and grapefruit juice in a mixing glass. Pour the preparation into a serving glass filled with the ice cubes and add the wheat beer. Garnish.

FOR THE GARNISH

fresh raspberries

RASPBERRY LIQUEUR WITH MAKRUT LIME OIL

400 ml (13 fl oz) raspberry liqueur • 1 drop of makrut lime essential oil

Mix the raspberry liqueur with the makrut lime essential oil.
Will keep at room temperature indefinitely.

MISTURA

Here is an amazing cocktail where I have combined the flavours of dried apricot with the slightly minty freshness of huacatay.

Makes 1 glass

50 ml (3 tablespoons) homemade white Lillet with dried apricots
15 ml (1 tablespoon) verjuice
5 large ice cubes
90 ml (3 fl oz) homemade huacatay soda

RECIPE

Mix the Lillet and verjuice in a mixing glass. Pour into a serving glass filled with the ice cubes, then add the huacatay soda. Garnish.

FOR THE GARNISH

2 slices of dried apricot
hucatay leaf

WHITE LILLET WITH DRIED APRICOTS

200 ml (7 fl oz) white Lillet • 50 g (2 oz) dried apricots

Make a cold infusion: let the Lillet and apricots infuse at room temperature for 3 days, then double strain.
Will keep at room temperature indefinitely.

HUACATAY SODA

4 g (1 teaspoon) dried or powdered huacatay
500 ml (17 fl oz) mineral water

Make a cold infusion: leave the huacatay to infuse in the water in the fridge for 24 hours. Strain, then gasify with a soda syphon.
Will keep in the fridge for 1 week maximum.

Focus on the Timur Berry

What is it?   The Timur berry, also known as 'grapefruit pepper', comes from a thorny plant of the citrus family. It grows naturally in the Mahābhārat Range mountains, at over 2,000 metres' (6,562 feet) altitude. It is the staple pepper among the people of the Terai, a humid region in southern Nepal, where you can find it in every kitchen, just like salt.

Did you know?   People often confuse the Timur berry and Timut pepper. They are actually one and the same. The berry is a relative of the Sichuan pepper, which is more widespread. In France, it's called Timut and in its native Nepal it is pronounced 'Timooor', but it's the same plant.

Its flavour in three words   Grapefruit + crystallised lemon + spicy.

How I use it   I very much like the citrus tones of this berry and use it in infusions. Its powerful aroma adds a pleasant bitterness to cocktails. It's often hard to guess straight away what it is... and I also like this element of surprise. Do not hesitate to crush the berries before making a cold or hot infusion, and, above all, do not let them infuse for too long (between 30 minutes and 1 hour maximum).

The Monin-Paragon brand offers a very good quality Timur berry cordial (a cordial is sweet and sour syrup, see page 143).

My other favourite peppers   I also very much like passion berries (from Ethiopia) and sansho (from Japan), with hints of citrus and mint. For me they are two essential peppers because they have very complementary fruity notes and take you on a unique journey of flavours.

AFRICAN STROLL

In this cocktail, I wanted you to sample the originality of emblematic African products, like bissap and yohimbe bark – I'll leave their virtues to your imagination.

Makes 1 glass

10 ml (⅔ tablespoon) rue berry cordial (Monin-Paragon brand)
100 ml (3½ fl oz) bissap juice
80 ml (2⅔ fl oz) homemade yohimbe bark soda
10 ml (⅔ tablespoon) agave syrup
5 large ice cubes

RECIPE

Pour all the ingredients into a glass. Garnish.

FOR THE GARNISH

crystallised hibiscus flowers

YOHIMBE BARK SODA

500 ml (17 fl oz) mineral water • 10 g (½ oz) yohimbe bark

Put the water and yohimbe bark into a saucepan. Bring to the boil, then infuse for 5 minutes. Remove the pan from the heat, double strain and allow to cool.
   Will keep in the fridge for 1 week maximum.

MASSALA TAJ

Here is a blend bursting with flavours. India inspired this effervescent cocktail, made even more exotic by the floral aromas of Martini.

Makes 1 glass

20 ml (1½ tablespoons) homemade massala chai syrup
50 ml (3 tablespoons) Martini Floreale (alcohol-free)
10 ml (⅔ tablespoon) verjuice
60 ml (2 fl oz) Badoit Rouge Intense (intensely carbonated)
5 large ice cubes

RECIPE

Pour all the ingredients into a glass. Garnish.

FOR THE GARNISH

poppadom, broken into pieces

MASSALA CHAI SYRUP

100 ml (3½ fl oz) mineral water • 5 g (1¼ teaspoons) chai tea • 100 g (3½ oz) caster (superfine) sugar

Heat the water to 80°C (180°F) and add the tea. Infuse for 15 minutes at 60°C (140°F), then add the sugar, stir and allow to cool.

Will keep at room temperature for 2 weeks maximum.

COLD MONO- AND MULTI-INFUSIONS WITH OR WITHOUT ALCOHOL

I think cold infusions are very important for capturing all the aroma molecules in nature by tampering as little as possible with the raw product. Time does all the work.

Beware: when using ingredients like (bell) peppers, chillies or teas, taste your infusions regularly, because, as you will see in this book, some infusions take only 30 minutes, others between 24 and 72 hours.

For example, I make a cold mono-infusion (also called maceration) in alcohol for the cocktail Parfum de France (page 103) with blackcurrant liqueur and dried verbena, and a cold multi-infusion without alcohol for Red Lemonade (page 94), with mineral water, ginger, lemon and dried hibiscus.

THE WATCHMAKERS

Gentian is quite a common mountain herb in Switzerland. Its bitter taste counterbalances the taste of the apple, which, combined with dry, fruity white wine, makes quite a complex drink.

Makes 1 glass

5 ml (1 teaspoon) gentian liqueur
20 ml (1½ tablespoons) homemade apple liqueur infused with wild lime tree leaves
80 ml (2⅔ fl oz) white wine (dry and fruity)
10 ml (⅔ tablespoon) verjuice

RECIPE

Pour all the ingredients into a mixing glass. Stir and strain into a serving glass. Garnish.

FOR THE GARNISH

fresh lime tree leaves

APPLE LIQUEUR INFUSED WITH WILD LIME TREE LEAVES

10 g (½ oz) dried lime tree leaves • 200 ml (7 fl oz) apple liqueur

Make a cold infusion: place the lime tree leaves in the apple liqueur and infuse at room temperature for 24 hours, then strain.
Will keep at room temperature indefinitely.

CÉRÈS BROTHERS

The Greek soul is at the heart of this enchanting cocktail. Take your time to enjoy the unusual flavour of mastika, the natural resin widely available in Greece, well known to the natives...

Makes 1 glass

15 ml (1 tablespoon) homemade mastika syrup
60 ml (2 fl oz) Greek mountain tea (Kalios brand) infusion
90 ml (3 fl oz) grapefruit juice
10 ml (⅔ tablespoon) lemon juice
5 large ice cubes

RECIPE

Pour all the ingredients into the glass. Garnish.

FOR THE GARNISH

grapefruit slices
mountain tea

MASTIKA SYRUP

100 ml (3½ fl oz) mineral water • 100 g (3½ oz) caster (superfine) sugar • 5 g (1¼ teaspoons) mastika powder

Bring the water to the boil in a saucepan and add the sugar. Keep boiling until you obtain a syrup. Remove the pan from the heat and add the mastika powder. Whisk to blend well and allow to cool.

Will keep at room temperature for 2 weeks maximum.

BASQUE SNACK

Even better if you can say it with a Basque accent. I invite you to discover this apple-pepper combination from the French town Espelette, in a cocktail that is at once subtle and spicy. By the way, do you know Espelette?

Makes 1 glass

90 ml (3 fl oz) homemade apple juice infused with Espelette pepper
10 ml (⅔ tablespoon) verjuice
10 ml (⅔ tablespoon) flower honey
5 large ice cubes
90 ml (3 fl oz) alcohol-free beer

RECIPE

Pour all the ingredients, except the beer (you'll add that at the last minute), into the glass. Garnish.

FOR THE GARNISH

1 teaspoon finely chopped Espelette pepper

APPLE JUICE INFUSED WITH ESPELETTE PEPPER

3 g (¾ teaspoon) Espelette pepper • 500 ml (17 fl oz) good-quality organic apple juice

Make a cold infusion: put the Espelette pepper into the apple juice and infuse for 30 minutes at room temperature, then strain.

Will keep in the fridge for 1 week maximum.

AFTERNOON SNACK TIME

FROM 4 P.M. TO 6 P.M.

A well-earnt sweet break

A CLOUD OF MADELEINE

The madeleine of my childhood, of the breaks at my school desk... or of when you feel peckish at around 4... The madeleine is everywhere, ready to be mischievously enjoyed.

Makes 1 glass

30 ml (1 fl oz) Routin Dry vermouth
50 ml (3 tablespoons) St Raphaël Classic Amber
10 ml (⅔ tablespoon) verjuice
4–6 large ice cubes
homemade oat milk and madeleine foam

RECIPE

Pour all the ingredients, except the foam, into a mixing glass. Stir with the ice cubes and strain, without the ice, then add the foam just before serving. Garnish.

FOR THE GARNISH

madeleine crumbs

OAT MILK AND MADELEINE FOAM

400 ml (13 fl oz) oat milk · 30 ml (1 fl oz) madeleine syrup (Routin brand)

Pour the milk and syrup into a syphon. Use one gas cartridge to make the foam.
  Will keep in the fridge for 3 days maximum.

LA BELLE HÉLÈNE

The very mention of this dessert makes your mouth water. Here is a liquid version, devised around a fruit I love: the pear... like a memory of desserts from bygone times...

Makes 1 glass

6–8 large ice cubes
80 ml (2⅔ fl oz) homemade green tea with pear
30 ml (1 fl oz) dark chocolate liqueur
120 ml (4 fl oz) pear cider

RECIPE

Put a few of the ice cubes into a glass, add the green tea and chocolate liqueur. Stir, then complete with the pear cider and remaining ice cubes. Garnish.

FOR THE GARNISH

fresh pear segments

GREEN TEA WITH PEAR

8 g (2 teaspoons) green tea with pear • 200 ml (7 fl oz) mineral water

Put the tea into a carafe with the water and leave to infuse in the fridge for 24 hours. Strain before use.
Will keep in the fridge for 1 week maximum.

CITRUS AND TRADITION

As you know, I am fond of citrus fruits. Here, I propose a homemade lemonade in which the flavours of easily available fruits come together to create a highly aromatic drink.

Makes 1 glass

1 scoop of lemon sorbet
30 ml (1 fl oz) bergamot liqueur
10 ml (⅔ tablespoon) lime juice
90 ml (3 fl oz) homemade clementine and Timur berry soda

RECIPE

Place the scoop of sorbet at the bottom of a glass, then add the liqueur and lime juice. Just before serving, add the soda. Garnish.

FOR THE GARNISH

1 small lemon leaf

CLEMENTINE AND TIMUR BERRY SODA

2 g (½ teaspoon) Timur berries • 200 ml (7 fl oz) clementine juice

Allow the Timur berries to infuse in the clementine juice in the fridge for 3 hours, then strain. Gasify the concoction with a soda syphon.

Will keep in the fridge for 1 week maximum.

RED BASKET

Summer, with its batch of red and black fruits, as well as the small glass of rosé wine on a late afternoon on a café terrace...: everything is aligned for a break: 100 per cent chill.

Makes 1 glass

4–6 large ice cubes
90 ml (3 fl oz) rosé wine
20 ml (1½ tablespoons) homemade wild strawberry and basil liqueur
10 ml (⅔ tablespoon) homemade blueberry and raspberry cordial
60 ml (2 fl oz) Badoit Rouge Intense

RECIPE

Put a few of the ice cubes into a glass and add the other ingredients, except the Badoit. Mix and complete with the Badoit and the remaining ice cubes. Garnish.

FOR THE GARNISH

fresh fruit (such as raspberries, blueberries, strawberries)

WILD STRAWBERRY AND BASIL LIQUEUR

8 g (2 teaspoons) dried basil • 200 ml (7 fl oz) strawberry liqueur

Pour the basil and liqueur into a carafe and leave to infuse at room temperature for 24 hours. Strain before use.
   Will keep at room temperature indefinitely.

BLUEBERRY AND RASPBERRY CORDIAL

150 ml (5 fl oz) blueberry purée • 150 ml (5 fl oz) raspberry purée • 200 g (7 oz) caster (superfine) sugar 100 ml (3½ fl oz) mineral water • 4 g (1 teaspoon) citric acid

Mix the fruit purées well with the sugar and water in a carafe. Add the citric acid and put aside. Strain.
   Will keep in the fridge for 1 week maximum.

LONDON TIME

'Afternoon snack' always makes one think of tea time, so a stop in London is mandatory. Let's go for a very British cocktail with notes of bitter orange and, naturally, my dear, Earl Grey tea.

Makes 1 glass

4–6 large ice cubes
60 ml (2 fl oz) apple juice
10 ml (⅔ tablespoon) lemon juice
1 teaspoon bitter orange marmalade
100 ml (3½ fl oz) homemade Earl Grey tea soda

RECIPE

Put the ice cubes into a glass, then add all the ingredients except the soda. Stir gently, pour in the soda and garnish.

FOR THE GARNISH

1 thin slice of fresh apricot
2 slivers of dried apricot

EARL GREY TEA SODA

5 g (1¼ teaspoons) Earl Grey tea • 500 ml (17 fl oz) mineral water

Put the tea in a carafe with the water and leave to infuse in the fridge for 24 hours. Strain, transfer to a soda syphon and gasify.
Will keep in the fridge for 1 week maximum.

PEACH SOBACHA

An invitation to a refreshing break thanks to the peach and the notes of roasted buckwheat.

Makes 1 glass

10 ml (⅔ tablespoon) lemon juice
30 ml (1 fl oz) homemade peach and buckwheat liqueur
60 ml (2 fl oz) apple juice
4–6 large ice cubes
120 ml (4 fl oz) wheat beer

RECIPE

Pour the lemon juice, peach liqueur and apple juice into a glass filled with the ice cubes. Stir, add the beer and stir again. Garnish.

FOR THE GARNISH

sliver of peach

PEACH AND BUCKWHEAT LIQUEUR

200 ml (7 fl oz) peach liqueur • 3 g (¾ teaspoon) buckwheat

Pour the peach liqueur and buckwheat into a carafe. Leave to infuse at room temperature for 24 hours, then strain.

Will keep at room temperature indefinitely.

MAKING NON-DAIRY MILK FOAM

We have long been making foam with cow's milk, cream and egg whites. Now we have the opportunity to create foams with some non-dairy milks, like oat or almond milk. All you need is a milk frother or a whisk.

Do not hesitate to try a plain version or a flavoured one, like in the recipes for Iced Salt Caramel Macchiato (page 19) and Cloud of Flavour (page 30). The goal is to give your cocktails a double texture with a light foam and a liquid.

CHOCO-COCO

The reflex afternoon snack is chocolate. I won't go against that, and am offering you a cocktail version of this concoction, light and subtle thanks to the almond-coconut foam.

Makes 1 glass

50 g (2 oz) dark chocolate
150 ml (5 fl oz) coconut milk
homemade almond and coconut foam

RECIPE

Melt the dark chocolate then pour it into a shaker with the coconut milk. Shake. Double strain into a glass and add the foam. Garnish (make the shavings with a bar of chocolate and a peeler). You can serve this drink hot or cold.

FOR THE GARNISH

cocoa powder
chocolate shavings

ALMOND AND COCONUT FOAM

300 ml (10 fl oz) almond milk • 100 ml (3½ fl oz) single (light) cream • 100 ml (3½ fl oz) coconut purée

Pour all the ingredients into a syphon. Use 1 gas cartridge to make the foam.
    Will keep in the fridge for 3 days maximum.

TRAVEL BREAK

You leave the office, take public transport, get stuck in traffic jams... then you finally get home just in time to enjoy this cocktail that heralds a gentle, relaxing evening.

Makes 1 glass

6–8 large ice cubes
50 ml (3 tablespoons) apricot nectar
15 ml (1 tablespoon) homemade rooibos and vanilla syrup
1 teaspoon orange blossom water
90 ml (3 fl oz) ginger kombucha

RECIPE

Put a few of the ice cubes into a glass and add all the other ingredients minus the kombucha. Stir, then add the kombucha and remaining ice cubes. Garnish.

FOR THE GARNISH

vanilla-flavoured rooibos tea leaves

ROOIBOS AND VANILLA SYRUP

100 g (3½ oz) caster (superfine) sugar
100 ml (3½ fl oz) mineral water • 3 g (¾ teaspoon) rooibos tea

Mix the sugar with the water and bring to the boil in a saucepan until you have obtained a syrup. Remove the pan from the heat and add the rooibos tea. Cover with a lid and leave to infuse at room temperature for 2 hours. Strain before use.
Will keep at room temperature for 2 weeks maximum.

RED LEMONADE

An elixir of coolness... there's nothing else to say.

Makes 1 glass

150 ml (5 fl oz) homemade lemon, hibiscus and ginger infusion
30 ml (1 fl oz) homemade pink grapefruit cordial
10 ml (⅔ tablespoon) lime juice
4–6 large ice cubes

RECIPE

Pour all the ingredients, minus the ice cubes, into a shaker. Shake, then transfer into a glass filled with the ice cubes. Garnish.

FOR THE GARNISH

slices of grapefruit and lemon

LEMON, HIBISCUS AND GINGER INFUSION

*3 g (¾ teaspoon) powdered (or leaf) hibiscus
2 g (½ teaspoon) fresh ginger • 50 g (2 oz) (whole)
organic lemon • 500 ml (17 fl oz) mineral water*

Put all the ingredients into a carafe with the water and infuse at room temperature for 24 hours. Strain before use.
Will keep in the fridge for 1 week maximum.

PINK GRAPEFRUIT CORDIAL

*100 ml (3½ fl oz) pink grapefruit juice • 20 g (¾ oz)
pink grapefruit zest • 100 g (3½ oz) white caster
(superfine) sugar • 100 ml (3½ fl oz) mineral water*

Mix all the ingredients in a carafe. Strain.
Will keep at room temperature for 2 weeks maximum.

Focus on
Chamomile

What is it?   Roman chamomile – usually just called chamomile – is a small perennial herb. It is widely used in cooking and in evening teas, in medicine and cosmetics. It has many virtues: it is an anti-inflammatory and soothes minor mouth infections. There are several varieties of chamomile, including German chamomile, which is also frequently used in cooking.

Did you know?   The most unusual use of chamomile infusion is still the one that consists of washing your hands in it before starting a card game to increase your chances of winning!

Its flavour in three words   Bitter + intense + floral.

How I use it   Naturally, I use it as an infusion, though not necessarily a hot one (I then call it maceration). It goes very well with raspberries in Brunch Bubbles (page 40). The raspberries tone down the bitterness and make it sweeter. This cordial is also perfect for flavouring biscuits.

My other favourite flowers   Citrus flowers are amazing. They are not all good or edible. One of the best-known and truly bewitching is orange blossom, which is an invitation to travel. I also like osmanthus flower, which I use in particular in the Oriental Stroll cocktail (page 113) with apple juice and makrut lime. It's the perfect combination of flowers, fruits and leaves.

SUN INFINITY

Late afternoons in winter are always a little demoralising... Night falls and the sun hides far too quickly. To make up for that, this cocktail makes the day longer and promises warm nights.

Makes 1 glass

6–8 large ice cubes
40 ml (1¼ fl oz) passion fruit purée
20 ml (1½ tablespoons) homemade saffron honey
8 drops of green mint hydrolate
120 ml (4 fl oz) homemade chamomile soda
2 cinnamon sticks

RECIPE

Put a few of the ice cubes into a glass, then add the passion fruit purée, saffron honey and mint hydrolate. Stir before adding the chamomile soda. Garnish. Just before serving, smoke the glass with the cinnamon sticks (all my smoking tips are on page 119).

FOR THE GARNISH

mango leather (see method on page 199)

SAFFRON HONEY

100 ml (3½ fl oz) mineral water • 100 ml (3½ fl oz) honey • 2 pistils of saffron

Heat the water to 80°C (180°F). Add honey and saffron and infuse at room temperature for 24 hours. Strain before use.

Will keep at room temperature for 2 weeks maximum.

CHAMOMILE SODA

6 g (1½ teaspoons) chamomile • 500 ml (17 fl oz) mineral water

Put the chamomile and water into a carafe and infuse in the fridge for 24 hours. Strain then gasify with a soda syphon.

Will keep in the fridge for 2 weeks maximum.

PRE-DINNER

FROM 7 P.M. TO 9 P.M.

Aperitifs for everyone!

PARFUM DE FRANCE

France, the country of my childhood... at the heart of lavender fields that paint the landscape of Provence purple. The fragrance of these flowers blended with the intense, sweet aroma of wine.

Makes 1 glass

50 ml (3 tablespoons) rosé wine
30 ml (1 fl oz) Lillet rosé
20 ml (1½ tablespoons) homemade crème de cassis with verbena
1 squirt of lavender aromatic water

RECIPE

Pour all the ingredients except the lavender aromatic water into a mixing glass and stir gently. Add the lavender aromatic water before serving. Garnish.

FOR THE GARNISH

fresh verbena leaves

CRÈME DE CASSIS WITH VERBENA

10 g (½ oz) fresh verbena leaves • 200 ml (7 fl oz) crème de cassis

Leave the verbena leaves to infuse in the crème de cassis for 24 hours, then strain.
Will keep at room temperature indefinitely.

ISLAND APERITIVO

Why have to choose between the exotic and the bitter when they can be combined? A round body, freshness and a touch of sourness are the perfect companions of this famous aperitif.

Makes 1 glass

80 ml (2⅔ fl oz) prosecco
60 ml (2 fl oz) homemade passion fruit soda
50 ml (3 tablespoons) homemade Aperol infused with dried mango
1 slice of grapefruit
4–6 large ice cubes

RECIPE

Pour all the ingredients into a glass with a few of the ice cubes and stir gently before topping up with the remaining ice cubes. Garnish.

FOR THE GARNISH

½ fresh mango, roughly chopped

PASSION FRUIT SODA

500 ml (17 fl oz) mineral water • 40 g (1½ oz) passion fruit flesh

Put the water and passion fruit into a carafe, stir and infuse in the fridge for 24 hours. Strain and gasify with a soda syphon.
  Will keep in the fridge for 1 week maximum.

APEROL INFUSED WITH DRIED MANGO

200 g (7 oz) fresh mango • 200 ml (7 fl oz) Aperol

Peel the mango and cut into slices. Put these into the Aperol and infuse at room temperature for 24 hours, then strain.
  Will keep at room temperature indefinitely.

APPLE TRIO

Sometimes sharp, often sweet, apples are not to be cast aside. Here is a combination worth trying – you'll be sorry if you don't.

Makes 1 glass

120 ml (4 fl oz) dry scrumpy cider
10 ml (⅔ tablespoon) homemade apple honey
30 ml (1 fl oz) homemade apple and sweet woodruff liqueur
4–6 large ice cubes

RECIPE

Pour all the ingredients and a few of the ice cubes into the glass and stir gently before adding the remaining ice cubes. Garnish.

FOR THE GARNISH

caramelised apple slices (see method on page 39)

APPLE HONEY

400 g (14 oz) apples of your choice • 100 ml (3½ fl oz) mineral water • 100 ml (3½ fl oz) flower honey

Peel and chop the apples. Stir the honey into the water heated to 80°C (180°F) (the temperature is important) and add the chopped apple. Infuse for 24 hours. Strain.
    Will keep in the fridge for 2 weeks maximum.

APPLE AND SWEET WOODRUFF LIQUEUR

200 ml (7 fl oz) apple liqueur • 10 g (½ oz) sweet woodruff (admittedly, not easy to find)

Infuse the apple liqueur with the sweet woodruff for 24 hours. Strain.
    Will keep at room temperature indefinitely.

THE WORLD
OF BARKS

Focus on
Muira Puama

What is it? It is a tree with a grey trunk, native to Brazil, near Rio Negro in the Amazon, in particular, where its root is used in traditional medicine. It has been included in Brazilian pharmacopoeia since the 1950s.

Did you know? This bark is still included in British pharmacopoeia (*British Herbal Pharmacopoeia*) for the treatment of dysentery... and erectile dysfunction. One translation of it is 'potency wood'!

Its flavour in three words Discreet + cocky + promising.

How I use it I use it to smoke cocktails. I like the smoking method I describe on page 119. Like sprays, it adds a touch of sophistication to the taste when you serve the cocktail. It's simple to do and the wow effect is guaranteed. Make sure, however, that you use the appropriate tools and don't burn yourself. You can also use it as a decoction in mineral water for homemade sodas that will bring a woody elegance to your cocktail-mixing experience.

My other favourite bark Quinquina bark is at the base of various famous 'tonics'. Do not hesitate to buy dried bark at the herbalist's and try decocting them. Don't forget apple tree bark, which should be grilled slightly and made as a cold infusion in various fruit juices.

KOALA SUNSET

Is there anything more beautiful than a fleeting, magical sunset in the land of koalas with a unique liquid experience that will transport you all the way to Australia?

Makes 1 glass

20 ml (1½ tablespoons) hibiscus syrup
60 ml (2 fl oz) alcohol-free white wine
4–6 large ice cubes
120 ml (4 fl oz) homemade passion fruit and eucalyptus soda

RECIPE

Pour the hibiscus and white wine into a glass with a few of the ice cubes, stir and add the remaining ice cubes before finishing with the passion fruit soda. Garnish.

FOR THE GARNISH

edible fresh leaves

PASSION FRUIT AND EUCALYPTUS SODA

50 g (2 oz) passion fruit flesh • 6 g (1½ teaspoons) dried eucalyptus leaves (from a herbalist)
500 ml (17 fl oz) mineral water

Put the passion fruit and eucalyptus into a carafe with the water and infuse in the fridge for 24 hours. Strain and gasify with a soda syphon.
Will keep in the fridge for 1 week maximum.

ORIENTAL STROLL

Deep in the rice fields, a brief encounter with the local villagers... sharing a smile and a cup of tea that has a sweet and sour fragrance.

Makes 1 glass

120 ml (4 fl oz) homemade sencha tea infusion
30 ml (1 fl oz) homemade osmanthus flower cordial
30 ml (1 fl oz) homemade Granny Smith apple purée

2 makrut lime leaves
4–6 large ice cubes

RECIPE

Put all the ingredients into a shaker, minus the ice cubes. Shake, then pour into a glass over the ice cubes. Garnish.

FOR THE GARNISH

makrut lime leaves

SENCHA TEA INFUSION

5 g (1¼ teaspoons) sencha tea • 500 ml (17 fl oz) mineral water

Put the tea into a carafe with the water and infuse in the fridge for 10 hours.

Will keep in the fridge for 1 week maximum.

GRANNY SMITH APPLE PURÉE

1 Granny Smith apple • lemon juice

Peel, core and chop the apple. Cook in a little water (1–2 tablespoons) on a low heat for 15 minutes. Add a drizzle of lemon juice when the cooking is complete. Leave to cool and stir roughly to obtain a purée. You can also stir for longer, to obtain a finer purée.

Will keep in the fridge for 1–2 days, as adding the drizzle of lemon juice will prevent it from darkening.

OSMANTHUS FLOWER CORDIAL

10 g (½ oz) dried osmanthus flowers • 100 ml (3½ fl oz) mineral water • 100 g (3½ oz) caster (superfine) sugar • 2 g (½ teaspoon) citric acid

Drop the osmanthus flowers into the water heated to 60–80°C (140–180°F) and infuse for 1 hour. Add the sugar and citric acid then stir. Strain.

Will keep at room temperature for 2 weeks maximum.

BITTER KISS

We're off around the world with this highly colourful trip. Allow yourself to be charmed by Italian intensity, French sweetness and a Nepalese experience in this red kiss.

Makes 1 glass

50 ml (3 tablespoons) St Raphael Le Quina Rouge
30 ml (1 fl oz) homemade tea liqueur infused with Timur berries
10 ml (⅔ tablespoon) Campari
4–6 large ice cubes

RECIPE

Pour all the ingredients into a glass filled with the ice cubes and stir gently. Garnish.

FOR THE GARNISH

orange peel

TEA INFUSED WITH TIMUR BERRIES LIQUEUR

3 g (¾ teaspoon) Timur berries • 200 ml (7 fl oz) tea liqueur

Infuse the Timur berries in the tea liqueur at room temperature for 1 hour, then strain.

Will keep at room temperature indefinitely.

SMOKING A COCKTAIL

Here is one of the simplest methods for smoking a cocktail: smoking the glass.

Place some cinnamon bark on a wooden board, burn it with a small blowtorch and immediately cover it with a glass. Wait 15–30 seconds. Fill the glass with ice cubes: the cold will fix the smoke to the glass. Then pour your chosen ingredients over the ice cubes.

Make sure you use the appropriate tools and be careful not to burn yourself.

Smoking can be used to add sophistication to a single-ingredient cocktail and also to obtain a smoky flavour.

You can use various bark essences or other dried ingredients, like hay, dried herbs, and so on.

RED SYLPH

Long nicknamed 'the devil's wine' because of its instability in the bottle, nowadays Champagne would deserve to be gently called 'angel wine'. Why not combine these two sides?

Makes 1 glass

4 large strawberries (Gariguette variety)
30 ml (1 fl oz) elderflower liqueur
5 ml (1 teaspoon) geranium hydrolate
4–6 large ice cubes
90 ml (3 fl oz) Champagne

RECIPE

Mash the strawberrries in a mixing glass and stir in the elderflower liqueur and geranium hydrolate. Add the ice cubes and stir. Double strain into a coupe glass and add the chilled Champagne. Garnish.

FOR THE GARNISH

strawberry leather (see method on page 199)

CITRUS TONIC

A little shot of energy to start the evening. A blend of citrus fruits with sharp, bitter and fruity flavours.

Makes 1 glass

60 ml (2 fl oz) homemade quinquina soda
50 ml (3 tablespoons) homemade green tea with bergamot
30 ml (1 fl oz) Seedlip Groove 42
15 ml (1 tablespoon) lemon juice
15 ml (1 tablespoon) agave syrup
5 ml (1 teaspoon) yuzu juice
4–6 large ice cubes

RECIPE

Pour all the ingredients and a few of the ice cubes into the glass and stir gently before adding the remaining ice cubes. Garnish.

FOR THE GARNISH

lemon slices

QUINQUINA SODA

2 g (½ teaspoon) quinquina bark • 500 ml (17 fl oz) mineral water

Boil the quinquina in the water for 5 minutes. Remove the saucepan from the heat, strain, and gasify with a soda syphon.
Will keep in the fridge for 1 week maximum.

GREEN TEA WITH BERGAMOT

5 g (1¼ teaspoons) green tea with bergamot 500 ml (17 fl oz) mineral water

Put the tea in a carafe with the water and infuse in the fridge for 24 hours, then strain.
Will keep in the fridge for 1 week maximum.

Focus on the Blackcurrant Leaf

What is it? It may sound a bit technical, but it is actually very simple. A hydrolate is an aromatic water obtained after the distillation of a natural raw material (when it is flowers, it is called 'floral water'). It is water resulting from the distillation that produces essential oil. Like my master perfumer friend Jean-Charles Sommerard, we can call it the 'memory' of distillation. With blackcurrants, you distil the leaves from the tree to draw out blackcurrant leaf essential oil on one hand, and distillate on the other. The same can be done with flowers, aromatic herbs, fruit, and so on.

Did you know? Blackcurrant leaf distillate has a dual action: it is both diuretic (often used in diets) and vasoprotective (for the circulatory system), which makes it beneficial for swollen legs. It also has a tonic and antioxidant effect on the skin.

Its flavour in three words Sweet + floral + fruity.

How I use it I use it in direct dilution in a glass or carafe. The advantage of hydrolates is that they dilute very easily in any ingredient, mineral water in particular, bringing a touch of nature without sugar. Blackcurrant leaves go very well with soft fruit and grapes.

My other favourite hydrolates I also love lavender and geranium hydrolates, or rather floral waters, which I use in particular in the Red Sylph (page 120) and Parfum de France (page 103) cocktails. These hydrolates have distinct, but gentle, herbal notes.

TITOU FRUITY PUNCH

Did you say punch? Yes, but without the punch. An original, exotic discovery that will surprise your taste buds.

Makes 1 glass

150 ml (5 fl oz) homemade pineapple juice infused with ginger
50 ml (3 tablespoons) alcohol-free whisky (Lyre's brand)
50 ml (3 tablespoons) mango juice
5 ml (1 teaspoon) orgeat syrup
4–6 large ice cubes

RECIPE

Pour all the ingredients into a shaker filled with the ice cubes and shake vigorously. Strain and serve without the ice cubes. Garnish.

FOR THE GARNISH

slices of pineapple, cherries or crystallised fruit

PINEAPPLE JUICE INFUSED WITH GINGER

500 ml (17 fl oz) fresh pineapple juice
5 g (1¼ teaspoons) dried ginger

Infuse the pineapple juice with the ginger for 12 hours. Strain.
    Will keep in the fridge for 1 week maximum.

EARLY EVENING

The sun is setting, the day is drawing to a close. What could be better than a moment of improvisation once the last file has been put away?

Makes 1 glass

50 ml (3 tablespoons) alcohol-free raspberry hydrolate (Fluère brand)
50 ml (3 tablespoons) cranberry juice
10 ml (⅔ tablespoon) homemade agave syrup infused with lemongrass
4–6 large ice cubes
90 ml (3 fl oz) alcohol-free beer

RECIPE

Pour all the ingredients, except the beer, into a glass with a few of the ice cubes. Stir gently before adding the remaining ice cubes and the beer.

AGAVE SYRUP INFUSED WITH LEMONGRASS

200 ml (7 fl oz) agave syrup • 1 drop of lemongrass essential oil

Mix the agave syrup with the lemongrass essential oil and keep at room temperature for 2 weeks maximum.

A LIQUID CHORD FOR AN EXQUISITE DINNER

FROM 9 P.M.

WATER LILY

A floating garden in the land of the rising sun. The perfect image to soothe us at the end of a long day.

Makes 1 glass

50 ml (3 tablespoons) homemade sake infused with sansho berries
20 ml (1½ tablespoons) umeshu (Japanese plum liqueur)
10 ml (⅔ tablespoon) verjuice
5 ml (1 teaspoon) homemade green tea and jasmine syrup
4–6 ice cubes

RECIPE

Pour all the ingredients into a mixing glass and add the ice cubes. Stir gently and transfer into a serving glass without the ice cubes. Garnish.

FOR THE GARNISH

oyster plant leaves (if you can find some!)

SAKE INFUSED WITH SANSHO BERRIES

200 ml (7 fl oz) Japanese sake • 1 g (¼ teaspoon) sansho berries

Pour the sake into a carafe with the berries and infuse at room temperature for 24 hours. Strain before serving.
Will keep at room temperature indefinitely.

GREEN TEA AND JASMINE SYRUP

100 ml (3½ fl oz) mineral water • 3 g (¾ teaspoon) green tea with jasmine • 100 g (3½ oz) caster (superfine) sugar

Bring the water to the boil and add the tea. Remove the saucepan from the stove and infuse for 1 hour. Add the sugar and put the pan back on a low heat to allow the sugar to dissolve slowly. The concoction must turn to syrup. Remove the pan from the heat, stir and strain.
Will keep in the fridge for 5 days maximum.

ASIAN MARKET

Pacing up and down the maze of a market, getting lost in the aisles and yielding to the temptation of a few smells and impromptu sampling.

Makes 1 glass

90 ml (3 fl oz) clear apple juice
40 ml (1¼ fl oz) sparkling water
20 ml (1½ tablespoons) lemon juice
20 ml (1½ tablespoons) homemade Batak berry cordial
6 Thai basil leaves
4–6 ice cubes

RECIPE

Pour all the ingredients into a shaker and add the ice cubes. Shake and double strain into a serving glass without the ice cubes. Garnish.

FOR THE GARNISH

Thai basil leaves

BATAK BERRY CORDIAL

100 ml (3½ fl oz) mineral water • 100 g (3½ oz) caster (superfine) sugar • 5 g (1¼ teaspoons) Batak berries • 2 g (½ teaspoon) citric acid

Heat the water in a saucepan and add the sugar. Bring to the boil and simmer until you obtain a syrup. Remove the pan from the heat, add the berries and infuse for 30 minutes. Strain and add the citric acid.

   Will keep at room temperature for 2 weeks maximum.

WILD RUBY

Red, impetuous and wild, like a ruby kept in secret. With its both subtle and honest flavours, it will surprise you and carry you away.

Makes 1 glass

80 ml (2⅔ fl oz) homemade raspberry and hibiscus infusion
50 ml (3 tablespoons) red grape juice
20 ml (1½ tablespoons) homemade rooibos and cherry cordial
10 ml (⅔ tablespoon) verjuice
6–8 large ice cubes

RECIPE

Pour all the ingredients into a glass with 5 of the ice cubes. Stir with a long spoon before adding the remaining ice cubes. Garnish.

FOR THE GARNISH

fresh cherries

RASPBERRY AND HIBISCUS INFUSION

200 g (7 oz) fresh raspberries • 500 ml (17 fl oz) mineral water • 5 g (1¼ teaspoons) dried hibiscus

Put the raspberries into a carafe with the water and add the dried hibiscus. Infuse in the fridge for 24 hours, then strain.
Will keep in the fridge for 1 week maximum.

ROOIBOS AND CHERRY CORDIAL

150 ml (5 fl oz) mineral water • 100 g (3½ oz) caster (superfine) sugar • 3 g (¾ teaspoon) rooibos tea with cherries • 2 g (½ teaspoon) citric acid

Heat the water in a saucepan and add the sugar. Bring to the boil and simmer until you have obtained a syrup. Remove the pan from the heat and infuse the rooibos tea for 20 minutes. Strain and add the citric acid.
Will keep at room temperature for 2 weeks maximum.

USING
A CORDIAL

The world of syrups is an integral part of French heritage. In France, we are lucky to still have master syrupers and be able to find excellent quality syrups.

In the world of mixology, a cordial is a less sweet syrup with a hint of sourness usually contributed by a natural citrus fruit, citric acid or other acids. You will see that I use them in many recipes, because, having obtained the sweet and sour balance, a cordial is usually simpler to integrate into no/low alcohol cocktails.

A reminder: a cordial is made with water, sugar, one or several products for infusing (fruit, flowers, leaves, and so on) and an acid.

NATURE DE FRANCE

Get out into the countryside! Rediscover the wonders of nature. Add a floral, fruity touch to rekindle a sweet, long-forgotten memory.

Makes 1 glass

80 ml (2⅔ fl oz) white grape juice
5 ml (1 teaspoon) blackcurrant hydrolate
20 ml (1½ tablespoons) verjuice
20 ml (1½ tablespoons) elderflower cordial
60 ml (2 fl oz) Badoit Rouge Intense
4–6 large ice cubes

RECIPE

Pour all the ingredients into a glass filled with the ice cubes. Add the Badoit at the last minute. Garnish.

FOR THE GARNISH

red grapes, cut into slices

CRUISE DOWN THE DANUBE

Let's stop off in Budapest, the city of a thousand and one lights.

Makes 1 glass

90 ml (3 fl oz) Hungarian Tokay wine
30 ml (1 fl oz) homemade blackcurrant liqueur with Hungarian paprika
10 ml (⅔ tablespoon) verjuice
4–6 large ice cubes

RECIPE

Pour all the ingredients into a mixing glass and add the ice cubes. Stir gently and strain into a serving glass without the ice cubes. Garnish.

FOR THE GARNISH

1 bay leaf

BLACKCURRANT LIQUEUR WITH HUNGARIAN PAPRIKA

200 ml (7 fl oz) blackcurrant liqueur • 2 g (½ teaspoon) Hungarian paprika

Pour the blackcurrant liqueur into a carafe, add the paprika and infuse at room temperature for 1 hour. Microstrain before use (paprika is very finely ground, so you need to use a very fine strainer).

Will keep at room temperature for 2 weeks maximum.

A VOYAGE SIGNATURE

How does this voyage begin? With a touch of the exotic, of tropical flavours and discoveries. This clarified cocktail will surprise you.

Makes 1 glass

80 ml (2⅔ fl oz) homemade pineapple and passion fruit mix
30 ml (1 fl oz) coconut cream
20 ml (1½ tablespoons) homemade muira puama bark syrup
20 ml (1½ tablespoons) lemon juice
50 ml (3 tablespoons) full-fat milk

RECIPE

Pour all the ingredients except the milk into a mixing glass. Pour the concoction over the milk (and – this is important – not the other way around) in another mixing glass. Stir and pour through a coffee filter into a large enough container. Once the liquid is clarified, keep in the fridge. Poor into a glass. Garnish.

FOR THE GARNISH

1 piece of pineapple

PINEAPPLE AND PASSION FRUIT MIX

300 ml (10 fl oz) fresh pineapple juice · 200 ml (7 fl oz) passion fruit purée

Pour the pineapple juice and passion fruit purée into a carafe, stir and set aside.
    Will keep in the fridge for 1 week maximum.

MUIRA PUAMA BARK SYRUP

100 ml (3½ fl oz) mineral water · 100 g (3½ oz) caster (superfine) sugar · 6 g (1½ teaspoons) muira puama bark

Heat the water in a saucepan and add the sugar. Bring to the boil and simmer until you obtain a syrup. Remove the pan from the heat and infuse the muira puama for 20 minutes. Strain.
    Will keep at room temperature for 2 weeks maximum.

THE WORLD OF
EDIBLE ESSENTIAL
OILS

Focus on the
Clementine

What is it? An essential oil is a liquid and aromatic extract generally obtained through the distillation of a plant through steam, which concentrates its volatile components. Once again, this may sound a little technical, but it is a way of obtaining the active properties of herbs. Like my perfumer friend Jean-Charles Sommerard, we can also call it the 'heart' of distillation.

Did you know? Clementine essential oil – like all essential oils – has many properties: antinauseant, diuretic, anticarcinogenic, but it is also very energising and mood-lifting – something we are very interested in in the cocktail world.

Its flavour in three words South + sweetness + bitterness (just enough).

How I use it I like using it to complement citrus in fruity and tonic recipes. It adds character... and you sometimes wonder what it is. Essential oil must be used sparingly and you must be sure it is edible. In general, one drop is enough to aromatise a 500 ml (17 fl oz) concoction. It is easily diluted in water-based ingredients like syrups or in honey.

My other favourite essential oils I like them all because the world of perfume is a personal inspiration. Combava (makrut lime peel) essential oil goes well with almond syrup, and ylang-ylang essential oil with agave syrup and fresh watermelon juice.

WHITE VALLEY

The Clare Valley: it stands between tradition and addiction.

Makes 1 glass

90 ml (3 fl oz) Australian Riesling
20 ml (1½ tablespoons) homemade apricot liqueur infused with Tasmanian pepperberries
10 ml (⅔ tablespoon) verjuice
4–6 ice cubes
eucalyptus spray

RECIPE

Pour all the ingredients into a glass and add the ice cubes. Stir gently and strain into a serving glass without the ice cubes. Spray the eucalyptus on top of the drink. Garnish.

FOR THE GARNISH

eucalyptus leaves

APRICOT LIQUEUR INFUSED WITH TASMANIAN PEPPERBERRIES

1 g (¼ teaspoon) Tasmanian pepperberries
200 ml (7 fl oz) apricot liqueur

Crush the Tasmanian pepperberries with a mortar and pestle. Add them to the apricot liqueur and infuse at room temperature for 24 hours. Strain before use.
    Will keep at room temperature indefinitely.

TRAMONTO

The dolce vita and a sunset in Portofino. That's all.

Makes 1 glass

4–6 large ice cubes
50 ml (3 tablespoons) red vermouth
10 ml (⅔ tablespoon) limoncello
90 ml (3 fl oz) Lambrusco

RECIPE

Fill a glass with the ice cubes, then pour in the vermouth and limoncello. Add the Lambrusco and a few more ice cubes if necessary. Garnish. To be enjoyed immediately.

FOR THE GARNISH

1 organic lemon peel

GOLDEN STAR

It shines brighter than the others after the sun has set. It dazzles you with its both sweet and herbal notes.

Makes 1 glass

5 ml (1 teaspoon) pine needle hydrolate
30 ml (1 fl oz) alcohol-free white vermouth (Martini Floreale brand)
60 ml (2 fl oz) clementine juice
4–6 large ice cubes
120 ml (4 fl oz) Badoit Rouge Intense

RECIPE

Pour the pine needle hydrolate, vermouth and clementine juice into a glass filled with the ice cubes, then top up to the brim with the Badoit. Garnish.

FOR THE GARNISH

a few fresh clementine segments or a twig of pine

A MIDSUMMER NIGHT'S DREAM

Let us head to the Champagne region, long enough for a stroll in the vineyards.

Makes 1 glass

30 ml (1 fl oz) pêche de vigne cream
5 ml (1 teaspoon) rosemary hydrolate
90 ml (3 fl oz) extra-dry Champagne
10 ml (⅔ tablespoon) verjuice
homemade Champagne foam

RECIPE

Pour the pêche de vigne cream and rosemary hydrolate into a mixing glass and strain it into a serving glass. Add the Champagne, verjuice and a little foam. Garnish.

FOR THE GARNISH

1 gold leaf

CHAMPAGNE FOAM

250 ml (8½ fl oz) Champagne • 150 ml (5 fl oz) full-fat milk • 100 ml (3½ fl oz) full-fat single (light) cream

Uncork a bottle of Champagne, help yourself to a glass and let all the bubbles out by stirring vigorously with a spoon. Add the milk and cream, then pour the concoction into a syphon. Use 1 gas cartridge to obtain a delicate foam.

Will keep in the fridge for 3 days maximum.

NIGHT SHIFT

FROM MIDNIGHT TO THE SMALL HOURS...

The classics – in new versions

CITRUS TONIC

There is still time to enjoy the night with passion and energy. Fall for this revisited classic.

Makes 1 glass

4 fresh kumquats
4–6 large ice cubes
30 ml (1 fl oz) homemade limoncello with juniper berries
15 ml (1 tablespoon) Timur berry cordial (Monin-Paragon brand)
120 ml (4 fl oz) tonic water

RECIPE

Crush the kumquats in a glass and fill with the ice cubes. Add the limoncello and Timur berry cordial. Finish with the tonic water and garnish.

FOR THE GARNISH

kumquat slices

LIMONCELLO WITH JUNIPER BERRIES

6 g (1½ teaspoons) juniper berries • 200 ml (7 fl oz) limoncello

Put the ingredients into a jar and infuse at room temperature for 24 hours. Strain before serving. Will keep at room temperature indefinitely.

ASIAN NIGHT

Again, the beautiful energy of Oriental cities, by day and by night. Here, you have the key flavours of lychees, rice and yuzu.

Makes 1 glass

4–6 large ice cubes
60 ml (2 fl oz) homemade lychee juice with dried rose
40 ml (1¼ fl oz) basmati rice water
90 ml (3 fl oz) homemade soda with yuzu peel

RECIPE

Fill the glass with the ice cubes, then add the lychee juice with rose and the rice water. Add the soda with yuzu peel and stir gently. Garnish.

FOR THE GARNISH

rose petals

LYCHEE JUICE WITH DRIED ROSE

200 ml (7 fl oz) lychee juice • 5 g (1¼ teaspoons) dried rose

Put the ingredients into a jar, close it and infuse at room temperature for 24 hours. Strain before serving.
Will keep in the fridge for 1 week maximum.

SODA WITH YUZU PEEL

500 ml (17 fl oz) mineral water • 15 g (½ oz) yuzu peel

Put the ingredients into a jar, close it and infuse in the fridge for 24 hours. Double strain and gasify with a soda syphon.
Will keep in the fridge for 1 week maximum.

HOMEMADE SODAS

Homemade sodas are currently my greatest inspiration when creating liquid experiments in the no/low world. Gasifying a drink gives cocktails an elegant complexity and makes it possible to have 100 per cent natural mono-experiences with as much sugar as you wish (concoctions with simple ingredients or sometimes even just one ingredient, without needing to mix several substances to obtain a good taste).

To create homemade sodas, you need equipment. Buy a small, good-quality soda syphon that will help you make these sparkling drinks easily. Make sure this isn't a kitchen syphon – they don't use the same gas cartridges. Soda syphons are often called Seltzer soda syphons.

Homemade soda is so easy to make for all your concoctions.

RED MOJITO

It's the same old tune as in Citrus Tonic... Who has never fallen for a mojito in the middle of the night? What I offer you here is a passion-red version.

Makes 1 glass

4–6 large ice cubes
30 ml (1 fl oz) cranberry juice
20 ml (1½ tablespoons) raspberry liqueur
10 ml (⅔ tablespoon) crème de cassis
juice of ½ lime
1 twig of fresh mint
4 whole strawberries
60 ml (2 fl oz) hibiscus and rose kombucha

RECIPE

Pour all the ingredients, except the kombucha, into a shaker. Shake and double strain into a glass, add the kombucha and stir. Garnish.

FOR THE GARNISH

mint leaves

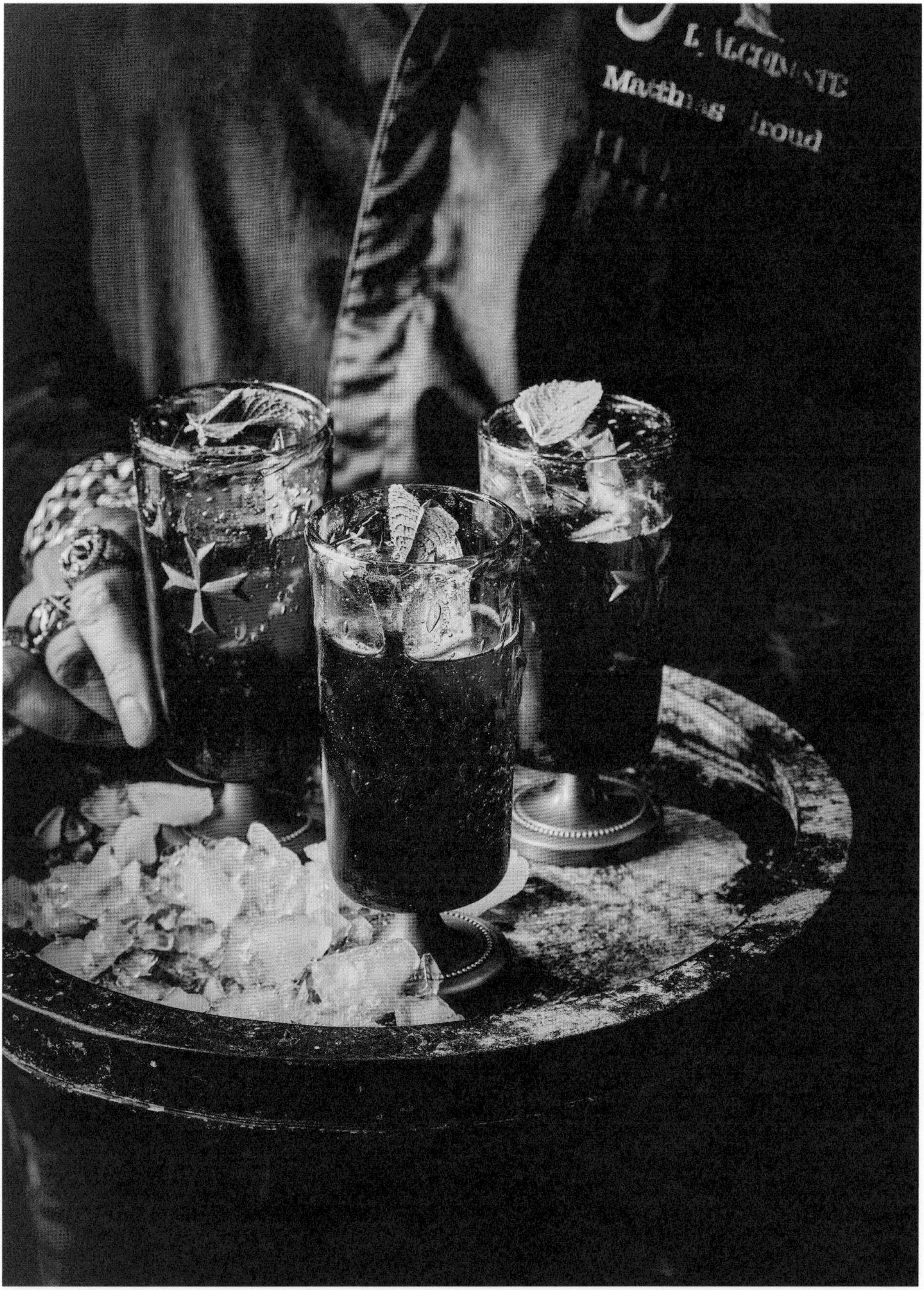
Matthias

PUNCH LOW PUNCH

Ah... This classic for exotic nights. Let yourself be tempted by the gentleness of almonds and the sweetness of pineapple.

Makes 1 glass

20 ml (1½ tablespoons) cherry liqueur
10 ml (⅔ tablespoon) homemade almond and pineapple liqueur
90 ml (3 fl oz) passion fruit juice
10 ml (⅔ tablespoon) lime juice
4–6 large ice cubes

RECIPE

Pour all the ingredients into a shaker. Shake and double strain into a serving glass.

ALMOND AND PINEAPPLE LIQUEUR

200 ml (7 fl oz) almond liqueur • 50 g (2 oz) fresh pineapple chunks

Put the ingredients into a jar, close it and infuse at room temperature for 24 hours. Strain before use.
Will keep at room temperature indefinitely.

LOW FASHIONED

Do you know Pineau des Charentes? I suggest you try it mixed with an old aperitif that is making a glamorous comeback: the Suze.

Makes 1 glass

60 ml (2 fl oz) homemade Pineau des Charentes with dried fig
20 ml (1½ tablespoons) homemade Suze with dried apricot
2 drops of orange bitters
4–6 large ice cubes

RECIPE

Pour all the ingredients into a glass and stir gently. Garnish.

FOR THE GARNISH

citrus fruit peel, cut up roughly (like in the photo opposite)

PINEAU DE CHARENTES WITH DRIED FIG

200 ml (7 fl oz) Pineau des Charentes • 20 g (¾ oz) dried figs

Put all the ingredients into a jar, close it and infuse at room temperature for 24 hours. Strain before use.
    Will keep at room temperature indefinitely.

SUZE WITH DRIED APRICOT

200 ml (7 fl oz) Suze • 20 g (¾ oz) dried apricot

Put the ingredients into a jar, close it and infuse at room temperature for 24 hours. Strain before use.
    Will keep at room temperature indefinitely.

ALCHEMIST MULE

One of my signature cocktails to help you dance all night.

Makes 1 glass

juice of ½ lime
4–6 large ice cubes
30 ml (1 fl oz) homemade ginger and lime liqueur
10 ml (⅔ tablespoon) agave syrup
90 ml (3 fl oz) homemade muira puama bark soda

RECIPE

Pour the lime in a glass and add the ice cubes, then the ginger ad lime liqueur, agave syrup and muira puama bark soda. Stir and garnish.

FOR THE GARNISH

3 slices of fresh ginger

GINGER AND LIME LIQUEUR

200 ml (7 fl oz) ginger liqueur • 10 g (½ oz) lime peel

Put all the ingredients into a jar, close it and infuse at room temperature for 24 hours. Strain before use.
   Will keep at room temperature indefinitely.

MUIRA PUAMA BARK SODA

500 ml (17 fl oz) mineral water • 6 g (1½ teaspoons) muira puama bark

Pour the water into a saucepan and add the bark. Bring to the boil, remove from the heat and infuse for 5 minutes. Double strain, allow to cool, then gasify with a soda syphon.
   Will keep in the fridge for 1 week maximum.

THE GRAPE

AND ITS WORLD

Preamble   How could I compile a book about cocktails and matching them to dishes without mentioning grapes, which are not only the essence of our beloved emblematic French drink – wine – but are also an empire of incredible flavours and diversity? A few words to explain my views of these magical bunches of fruit.

What is it?   I don't think there's any need to tell you what grapes are. Perhaps I could talk about grape varieties and the wine-making process, but that's not the point. What I want to do is to illustrate the way I like to use grapes. I particularly use them a lot in aperitif cocktails in verjuice form. Verjuice is a sharp juice extracted from grapes that are still green. It can be used instead of vinegar and adds pleasantly sour notes, typical in cocktails. I find it ideal when wishing to highlight other wines in light cocktails like Nature de France (page 144) and Cruise Down the Danube (page 147).

Did you know?   Seven-one per cent of grapes produced are used for wine, 27 per cent as fresh fruit and 2 per cent for dried fruit. Grapes are principally made up of water (about 80 per cent), which makes them a low-calorie snack. But be careful not to overdo it!

The grape in three words   Sharp + plural + incredible.

How I use it   I like using it in different forms and it makes particular sense in no/low experiments because, as you can see, there are many concoctions based on grapes, like vermouth, wine, Champagne, sparkling wine in the low-alcohol section, and verjuice and grape juice in no-alcohol cocktails. I also like using red vine leaves in infusions.

SOFT TONIC

No doubt you're familiar with gin and tonic. What I propose here is a smoother version with a concoction I particularly like: Seedlip, an alcohol-free hydrolate.

Makes 1 glass

4–6 large ice cubes
50 ml (3 tablespoons) Seedlip Groove 42
10 ml (⅔ tablespoon) homemade lemon juice with juniper berries
10 ml (⅔ tablespoon) Timur berry cordial (Monin-Paragon brand)
90 ml (3 fl oz) tonic water

RECIPE

Fill a glass with ice cubes, then pour the Seedlip and the lemon juice with juniper berries into it. Add the Timur berry cordial and the tonic water. Stir and garnish.

FOR THE GARNISH

citrus fruit peel, cut into discs (like
    in the photo opposite)
rosemary sprigs

LEMON JUICE WITH JUNIPER BERRIES

10 g (½ oz) juniper berries 200 ml · (7 fl oz) lemon juice

Crush the juniper berries with a mortar and pestle, then pour them into the lemon juice. Infuse in the fridge for 24 hours, then double strain.
    Will keep at room temperature indefinitely.

THE WORLD
OF ROOTS

Focus on
Ginger

What is it? Ginger is a plant native to India, whose rootstock is used in cooking and traditional medicine. Root ginger is what you commonly call the pieces of rootstock now easily found in the shops. This plant is widely used in Eastern cuisine because of its spicy notes. It is also recommended for its antioxidant and digestive properties, as well as its benefits for the vascular system.

Did you know? If consumed in excessive amounts it can be irritating to the stomach. Moreover, it is known for its stimulating effects.

Its flavour in three words Lemony + spicy + pungent.

How I use it I love infusing it. In the Titou Fruity Punch (page 129), it is infused in fresh pineapple juice – a perfect combination. The sweetness of the pineapple is highlighted by the spiciness of the ginger. Moreover, the exotic origins of both ingredients are a perfect match. Do not hesitate to use dried ginger and make it into a cold infusion in fruit juice, or into a hot decoction with water to make a soda.

My other favourite roots Gentian root is also very interesting. I use it as a liqueur in The Watchmakers recipe (page 65) as a tribute to the Vallée de Joux, a cradle of exclusive watchmaking and a hideout of wild gentian. It is an incredible source of energy... so be ready to climb mountains! Only use it carefully, because it can be very bitter in excess.

SCAR PUNCH

Don't be afraid... everything becomes possible with this punch.

Makes 1 glass

90 ml (3 fl oz) homemade pineapple, rooibos and vanilla juice
60 ml (2 fl oz) banana juice
50 ml (1¾ fl oz) alcohol-free rum (Lyre's Dark Cane Spirit brand)
10 ml (⅔ tablespoon) coconut cream
4–6 large ice cubes

RECIPE

Pour all the ingredients except for the ice cubes into a shaker and shake. Fill a glass with the ice cubes and double strain. Garnish.

FOR THE GARNISH

yellow candy floss

PINEAPPLE, ROOIBOS AND VANILLA JUICE

500 ml (17 fl oz) pineapple juice • 4 g (1 teaspoon) vanilla-flavoured rooibos tea

Pour the pineapple juice into a carafe with the vanilla-flavoured rooibos, stir and infuse in the fridge for 24 hours. Strain before serving.
Will keep in the fridge for 1 week maximum.

ALMOND SOUR

It's sweet, it's smooth... It's a perfect finish to a lovely long night...

Makes 1 glass

50 ml (1¾ fl oz) alcohol-free almond liqueur (Lyre's brand amaretti)
20 ml (1½ tablespoons) lemon juice
20 ml (1½ tablespoons) orgeat syrup
1 egg white
4–6 large ice cubes

RECIPE

Pour all the ingredients into a shaker, shake and double strain before serving. Garnish.

FOR THE GARNISH

ground almonds

CHACHA SUNRISE

The early morning hues... the sun will soon rise and you are still in the middle of a festive night... It will be your perfect ally with its sweet and sour notes.

Makes 1 glass

4–6 large ice cubes
90 ml (3 fl oz) clementine juice
30 ml (1 fl oz) alcohol-free agave distillate (Fluère brand)
10 ml (⅔ tablespoon) homemade grenadine syrup

RECIPE

Pour all the ingredients into a serving glass. Stir and garnish.

FOR THE GARNISH

clementine leather (see method on page 199)

GRENADINE SYRUP

200 ml (7 fl oz) fresh pomegranate juice • 200 g (7 oz) caster (superfine) sugar

Put the ingredients into a saucepan, bring to the boil and simmer until you have obtained a syrup.
   Will keep at room temperature for 2 weeks maximum.

THE MIXOLOGIST'S LEXICON

Soda machine and soda syphon These appliances may look complex, but they are essential to many recipes. They make it possible to create homemade sodas, that is, aromatic or infused (with tea, cordial or herbs, and so on), as well as carbonated drinks. They also provide a fun way to break the norm – for instance, tea is seldom a sparkling drink, but why shouldn't it be? It is quite a sizeable investment, but it will equally allow you to make everyday sparkling water. You will also be in charge of sodas for children: no more commercial sodas with excess sugar.

Mixer and mixing spoon Obviously, this is a small accessory that is part of the mixologist's arsenal. Usually very long and thin, with a bowl part that looks like that of a moka spoon, the mixing spoon allows you to show off socially, but especially to reach the bottom of the serving or mixing glass. Still, I can assure you that a long teaspoon will also do if you do not wish to invest in this tool. However, let me tell you that cocktail kits found in shops often contain many small accessories, including a strainer and a mixing spoon.

Milk frother It is a simple little tool often popular among lovers of cappuccino and other hot milky drinks. It is a must-have for latte art, but also in mixology because it helps create creamy and frothy textures. It also makes it possible to heat the liquid and turn it into foam very quickly.

Strainer, fine sieve and cocktail strainer Essential tools for cocktail making. They come in many shapes and finishes. Make sure you have at least a medium-sized one that will help you in all your concoctions. And if you wish to go further, you will need four types:
• a 15 cm (6 in)-diameter strainer known as 'Japanese conical strainer'
• a cocktail strainer (very specific and useful)
• a so-called 'julep' strainer, for decanting the concoction from the mixing glass to the serving glass
• a fine strainer (with a single or double mesh) for various kinds of straining.

Shaker I am sure you immediately thought of a shaker when you bought this book. It is obviously one of the mixologist's key tools. It is not, however, necessarily used for all cocktails, since there are some that don't require shaking. I recommend you get a medium-sized one (500–700 ml/17–24 fl oz) which will help you make concoctions for one or two people maximum. The shaker, generally made of stainless steel, must help make the cocktail airy when you shake it with ice cubes.

Classic syphon Many of you already know and perhaps even have a syphon at home. It makes it possible to make froth (or espumas) for many cooking recipes. I suggest you also use it in a few basic concoctions. I would like to point out that it is better to use a good quality appliance and appropriate cartridges. Take care when using it. If you don't feel comfortable using one, you can, of course, buy these concoctions ready-made (like the chocolate foam in Puff in a Mug on page 22.

Spray   As you will see, I often use sprays to complete my cocktails. It is quite a simple method that makes it possible to add, for example, floral notes, to finish and give a super-fresh touch to a cocktail. Sprays are often used at the very end of the cocktail-making process, just before drinking. With their cool body language, they are all the rage. There are many kinds of sprays, easy enough to find, from the more modest transparent bottles (like Muji) to the more original ones you will find in luxury perfume shops.

I very much like using plant-based sprays to add a light tone just before serving. They are the first notes to present themselves even before the cocktail is sampled. They make it possible to approach the cocktail dreamily and voluptuously.

Be careful not to use the same spray for several concoctions, and especially not for cosmetics!

Mixing glass   There are a large number of models, in glass and stainless steel. Choose the one you like. Used with its spoon, it is great for mixing drinks that cannot be prepared in a shaker. Preparation in a mixing glass is gentler and preserves the flavour of every ingredient while ensuring they are blended thanks to the ice cubes.

Serving glasses   These truly are my darlings! As you can see in this book, serving glasses add something to the presentation and enjoyment of cocktails. There are hundreds of styles... and to prove it, I offer here 60 concoctions in 60 different glasses. When we talk about 'glasses' in mixology, we obviously mean those made of glass, but also ceramic, stainless steel, copper, porcelain, wood and even crystal containers. Anything is possible as long as you are being creative. All my cocktails are served in very original containers. I suspect you will not have exactly the same ones at home, which is why I suggest you follow your fancy and let your artistic sense speak.

METHODS AND TECHNIQUES

Straining and double straining You will often read the words 'strain' and 'double strain' in my recipes. When you prepare a syrup or an infusion, or macerate something, you mix the ingredients in a liquid (water, juice, syrup, alcohol, and so on). When the required time is over, the concoction must be made more fluid and the ingredients used removed. You therefore strain it. You also do so after shaking, before pouring the drink into a glass. This action can be performed with various tools. The simplest thing to do is to use a fine strainer that will help filter large quantities quickly. You can also use a cheesecloth for even finer straining. Another option, if you do not have the required materials, is to use an ordinary strainer coated with a piece of paper towel or a disposable coffee filter.

There are also some small strainers I mention in the chapter on tools (page 193) for straining small quantities just as you are serving. The important thing is to obtain a very fluid drink, freed from all the elements of the infusion, and, above all, one that is pleasant to drink. Now it's up to you!

Mixing I suggest you mix some concoctions to make them more homogenous. You can use equipment you already have at home: a hand blender (yes, the one you use for soup), a classic mixer or even a blender (on slow speed).

Infusion and maceration These two words are often confused or inverted. Here is some information to help you find your way around, but it's no big deal if you don't use the correct word.

Infusion consists of pouring boiling water on vegetable matter and leaving it to infuse for several minutes: it's the simple principle of tea making!

Maceration, on the other hand, consists of infusing a product in cold water for several hours. One then often calls it 'cold infusion', like in the Oriental Stroll (page 113) and Wild Ruby (page 140). The word 'macerate' may sound a bit scary because it naturally – and unfairly – suggests things that stay in water for too long. In the world of cocktails and cuisine, the maceration technique could be compared to a marinade. The word 'marinate' is chiefly used for animal matter (fish and meat), whereas for plants (fruit, vegetables and herbs) you say 'maceration'.

I hope you're reassured!

BASIC PREPARATIONS

Cordials   Cordials work on the same principle as syrups (a blend of water, sugar, and fruit or plants), but are less sweet and have a touch of sourness. They lift the cocktail and make it sharp. Their taste – stronger because they have less sugar – makes them into the ideal cocktail ingredient and not just a condiment.

Syrups   Syrups are an unmissable base of mixology. In this book, I offer many recipes for creating homemade syrups. They help obtain often less sugary blends than commercial ones. Thanks to them, you will make between 500 and 750 ml (17 and 25 fl oz) of syrup, which you can keep for other cocktails, or even for making sorbets and desserts for the little ones!

The base of the syrup is water and sugar. Fruit or plants are infused in it to bring aromatic complexity to the liquid. In general, we use 100 ml (3½ fl oz) of water for 30 to 50 g (1 to 2oz) of sugar and 10 to 20 g (½ to ¾ oz) of plant or fruit.

Fruit leather   Fruit 'leather' is my secret weapon. It is a kind of dried fruit (or herb) paste. You must first make a vegetable matter purée (like strawberries on page 120 or peach on page 36), which you then spread thinly on a sheet and put in the oven. It needs to be very thin. You then use the dehydration setting on the oven (or a dehydrator) for 6–8 hours at 45–50°C (110–120°F).

When you undertake this preparation, allow a sufficient quantity to make a small stock of it. Leathers don't keep very long (10–12 days), but you can use them to complete a dessert or brighten dry biscuits.

Ice cubes   Ah, the famous ice cubes! Now there's an important topic when making our lovely drinks.

Although not all cocktails require ice cubes – some deserve to be served cool but not diluted (that's right, ice cubes melt once they are mixed in) – it is better to be ready.

The base: water. Of course, you can make your ice cubes with tap water, but ideally with neutral mineral water – it is much better.

Then come the trays. And that is where you have a debate. It is hard to have at home splendid 5 cm (2 in) cubes like in the best bars. I suggest you buy a few ice-cube trays (they can be inexpensive on many websites) which will do the trick.

When serving, avoid small – under 2 cm (¾ in) – ice cubes, which melt quickly and do not add much to the recipe. They are only useful for basic mixes (in a mixing glass or shaker). When serving, it is better to choose large blocks. You can also find rectangular ice cubes that are stylish. Personally, I avoid ice cubes with shapes that are too complicated to push out or too 'gadgety'. It is up to you.

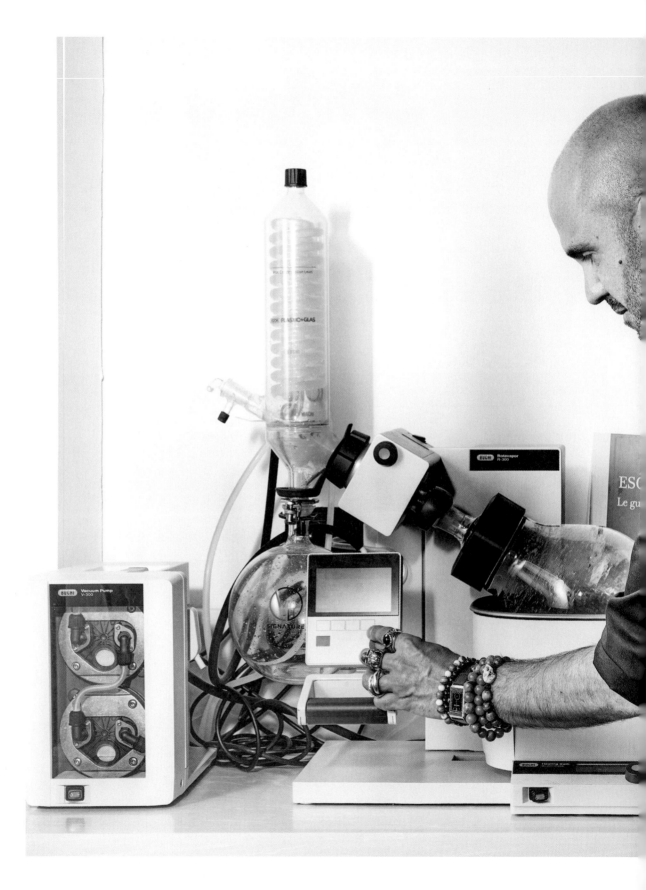

INDEX

Ingredients index

Pink Grapefruit Liqueur: Citrus Coffee 25
Raspberry Liqueur: Red Mojito 168; Sumbawa 53
Strawberry Liqueur: Red Basket 81
Tea Liqueur: Bitter Kiss 116
Umeshu (Japanese plum liqueur): Water Lily 137

SYRUPS & CREAMS

Agave Syrup: African Stroll 58; Alchemist Mule 176; Citrus Tonic 125; Early Evening 130; Japan Detox 35
Almond Syrup: Morning Himalaya 28
Coconut Cream: Scar Punch 184; A Voyage Signature 149
Crème de Cassis: Parfum de France 103; Red Mojito 168
Grenadine Syrup: Chacha Sunrise 188
Hibiscus Syrup: Koala Sunset 111
Jasmine Syrup: Water Lily 137
Madeline Syrup: A Cloud of Madeleine 73
Muira Puama Bark Syrup: A Voyage Signature 149
Orgeat Syrup: Almond Sour 187; Titou Fruity Punch 129
Pêche de Vigne Cream: A Midsummer Night's Dream 158
Salt Caramel Syrup: Iced Salt Caramel Macchiato 19

SWEET

Chocolate: Choco-Coco 89; Puff in a Mug 22
Honey: Apple Trio 106; Basque Snack 68; Rising Sun 15; Sun

Infinity 98
Lemon Sorbet: Citrus and Tradition 76
Orange Marmalade: London Time 83
Sugar: Asian Market 138; Brunch Bubbles 40; Cérès Brothers 66; Chacha Sunrise 188; Massala Taj 60; Oriental Stroll 113; Raspberry Charm 44; Red Basket 81; Red Lemonade 94; Sanova 48; Travel Break 93; A Voyage Signature 149; Water Lily 137; Wild Ruby 140

TEAS

Darjeeling: Morning Himalaya 28
Earl Grey: London Time 83
Greek Mountain Tea: Cérès Brothers 66
Green Tea: Citrus Tonic 125; Japan Detox 35; La Belle Hélène 74; Water Lily 137
Massala Chai: Massala Taj 60
Matcha Tea: Rising Sun 15
Rooibos: Alchemist Mule 176; Cloud of Flavour 30; Scar Punch 184; Travel Break 93
Sencha Tea: Oriental Stroll 113

WINES & SPIRITS

Aperol: Island Aperitivo 104
Campari: Bitter Kiss 116
Champagne: Brunch Bubbles 40; A Midsummer Night's Dream 158; Red Sylph 120
Cider: Apple Trio 106; French Bellini 36; La Belle Hélène 74
Lambrusco: Tramonto 154
Lillet Rosé: Parfum de France 103
Lillet White : Mistura 55

Pineau des Charentes: Low Fashioned 175
Prosecco: Island Aperitivo 104
Sake: Water Lily 137
St Raphaël: Bitter Kiss 116; A Cloud of Madeleine 73
Suze: Low Fashioned 175
Tokay Wine: Cruise Down the Danube 147
Umeshu : Water Lily 137
Vermouth: A Cloud of Madeleine 73; Golden Star 157; Sanova 48; Tramonto 154
Wheat Beer: Peach Sobacha 84; Sumbawa 53
Wine (Rosé): Parfum de France 103; Red Basket 81
Wine (White): Fleurs de France 47; The Watchmakers 65; White Valley 152

...AND MORE

Buckwheat: French Bellini 36; Peach Sobacha 84
Citric Acid: Asian Market 138; Oriental Stroll 113
Cream: Choco-Coco 89; A Midsummer Night's Dream 158
Egg White: Almond Sour 187
Kombucha (Ginger): Travel Break 93
Kombucha (Pomegranate): A Stroll Through the Palm Grove 16
Kombucha (Rose): Red Mojito 168

Address book

Essential oils and hydrolates
www.essenciagua.fr
An artisanal distillery based
in Provence
Or at good herbalists

palaisdesthes.com
and in many French cities

Peppers and spices
Terre Exotique is a widespread
brand in delicatessens
Also on the website
www.terreexotique.fr

Bark and peels
www.herboristerieduvalmont.com
Particularly for yohimbe

Candied and dried fruits and flowers
www.ileauxepices.com

Liqueurs
I quite like the brand
Marie Brizard
which is easy to find

Syrups
Monin brand
and **Routin** syrups

For very specific products
• Huacatay, a South American leaf
native to Peru:
www.boutique-peruvienne.com
• Cascara
www.cafepiha.com

Greek products
www.mykalios.com
For mastika powder, ask a Greek
friend or search online

Bergamot liqueur
Italicus brand
Easily available in delicatessens
or at wine merchants

Fruit purées and products specific to pastry making
www.cuisineaddict.com

Ice-cube trays
https://la-maison-du-barman.fr

Sweet woodruff and osmanthus flowers
From herbalists and in particular
www.calebasse.com

Citrus fruits and specific citrus leaves
From Asian delicatessens

Alcohol-free alcohol, like Seedlip, Fluère and Lyre's
www.drinksco.fr

Sakes and Japanese alcoholic drinks
www.atelierdusake.com
www.rioko.fr
Make sure you choose
Japanese sake!

Verjuice
Bourgoin brand

Limoncello
Bomba brand

206

Matthias Giroud's acknowledgements

The adventure of this book had been close to my heart for many seasons and I am truly delighted that it has come into the world. My first thanks therefore go to Solar and in particular Didier Férat and Diane Monserat. Thank you for believing in the project straight away and giving your time to bring it to life!

This encounter would not have happened without Anaïs Delon, my co-author, with whom I have shared a great deal in order to find the right balance between all the yens in my head.

Thanks to Valéry Guedes for his talent and his photographs, to Élisabeth Guedes for staging the recipes at any time of the day or night.

Thanks to my Alchimiste team for their involvement and their patience. For being actively on my side on all the projects.

Special thanks to my principal inspirations, nature – and in particular mountains – and my travels, with all the encounters I have had throughout the world.

Finally, to my darling Mélinda, my very special partner, my other half who is as complementary as she is different, who is as passionate as I am about bringing to life all these no/low alcohol creations into the world of bars, hospitality and restaurants, now and in the future.

Anaïs Delon's acknowledgements

Thanks to both Matthias and Mélinda for their trust, their energy and their friendship.

To Didier for his loyalty, and to Diane for her patience and her cheerfulness no matter what the challenge.

To Hugo Bourny for believing in me and all my projects (however varied!).

First published in the French language in 2022 originally under the title:
Cocktails No Low
© 2022, Editions Gründ, an imprint of Edi8, Paris

This English edition published in 2024 by Hardie Grant Books,
an imprint of Hardie Grant Publishing

Hardie Grant Books (London)
5th & 6th Floors
52–54 Southwark Street
London SE1 1UN

Hardie Grant Books (Melbourne)
Building 1, 658 Church Street
Richmond, Victoria 3121

hardiegrantbooks.com

British Library Cataloguing-in-Publication Data. A catalogue record for this book
is available from the British Library.

Low- and No-Alcohol Cocktails
ISBN: 978-178488-702-5

10 9 8 7 6 5 4 3 2 1

For the French edition:
Design: Moshi Moshi Studio
Photography and styling: Valéry Guedes and Élisabeth Guedes

For the English edition:
Publishing Director: Kajal Mistry
Commissioning Editor: Kate Burkett
Senior Editor: Eila Purvis
Translator: Katherine Gregor
Typesettor: David Meikle
Proofreader: Sue Juby
Production Controller: Martina Georgieva

Colour reproduction by p2d
Printed and bound in China by Leo Paper Products Ltd.